D0856703

MAP BASICS

TIME ZONES

BY RYAN NAGELHOUT

Gareth Stevens PUBLISHING

Please visit our website, www.garethstevens.com. For a free color catalog of all our high-quality books, call toll free 1-800-542-2595 or fax 1-877-542-2596.

Library of Congress Cataloging-in-Publication Data

Nagelhout, Ryan.
Time zones / by Ryan Nagelhout.
p. cm. — (Map basics)
Includes index.
ISBN 978-1-4824-1069-3 (pbk.)
ISBN 978-1-4824-1070-9 (6-pack)
ISBN 978-1-4824-1068-6 (library binding)
1. Time measurements — Juvenile literature. 2. Time — Systems and standards — Juvenile literature.
I. Nagelhout, Ryan. II. Title.
QB209.5 N34 2015
389—d23

First Edition

Published in 2015 by
Gareth Stevens Publishing
111 East 14th Street, Suite 349
New York, NY 10003

Designer: Sarah Liddell
Editor: Kristen Rajczak

Photo credits: Cover, p. 1 vso/Shutterstock.com; p. 5 B-A-C-O/Shutterstock.com; p. 7 Anders Blomqvist/Lonely Planet Images/Getty Images; p. 9 photo courtesy of the Library of Congress; p. 11 Rand McNally and Company/Wikimedia Commons; p. 13 dalmingo/Shutterstock.com; p. 15 Rainer Lesniewski/Shutterstock.com; p. 17 pavalena/Shutterstock.com; p. 19 JBOY/Shutterstock.com.

Printed in the United States of America

CPSIA compliance information: Batch #CS15GS: For further information contact Gareth Stevens, New York, New York at 1-800-542-2595.

CONTENTS

Words in the glossary appear in **bold** type the first time they are used in the text.

CLOCKING IN

What time is it where you live? What about in Paris, France? Earth is divided into time zones, or areas that have the same time. If you don't live in the same time zone as France, it isn't the same time.

Times zones help us keep clocks working together all around the world. They make traveling, talking, and doing business easier. Without time zones, no one would know what time it is anywhere else in the world!

JUST THE FACTS

Before time zones were established, many places would figure out the time based on when the sun was the highest in the sky, or noon.

BUENOS AIRES, ARGENTINA

SYDNEY, AUSTRALIA

LONDON, ENGLAND

NEW YORK CITY, USA

CAPE TOWN, SOUTH AFRICA

TOKYO, JAPAN

Post offices and some businesses have clocks showing different times all over the world.

TELLING TIME

For thousands of years, people living in different places kept time their own way. Some used water dripping out of a pot to measure time.

In 1656, timekeeping became more exact with the invention of the **pendulum** clock. But cities still kept their own time separate from one another. No one was moving between major cities fast enough to make uniform timekeeping necessary. A minute or even an hour here or there just wasn't important enough to track.

JUST THE FACTS

Christiaan Huygens invented the pendulum clock. It keeps time by the steady swinging of a pendulum back and forth. These clocks were the best and most exact way to measure time for almost 300 years!

Sundials like this one were early clocks, which used the sun to tell the time.

RAIL TROUBLE

During the 19th century, railroads made traveling long distances easier and faster. But knowing when trains would leave and arrive at two different places was impossible if the cities didn't keep the same time. In the United States, there were more than 300 local times used by different cities!

People trying to use the rail lines were often confused, and **schedules** were hard to make. Railroad managers created 100 railroad time zones to try to fix the problem.

JUST THE FACTS

By 1900, trains were traveling nearly 100 miles (161 km) per hour for long stretches of time. It was hard for passengers to keep track of where they were to know the time!

This map shows the many rail lines crisscrossing the United States in the 1800s.

RAILROAD TIME

The 100 railroad time zones only partly solved the problems with railroad schedules. Railroad companies met in 1883 to figure out how to make keeping time easier. They decided that the United States should be divided into four equal time zones.

Inside each time zone, there would be a set time that anyone inside the zone would use. This is called standard time.

Soon after, Great Britain and the United States helped plan the **global** time zones.

JUST THE FACTS

November 18, 1883, was called the "day of two noons," as the United States put standard time into effect. Everyone had to stop what they were doing and reset all their clocks and watches so they would have the new, right time.

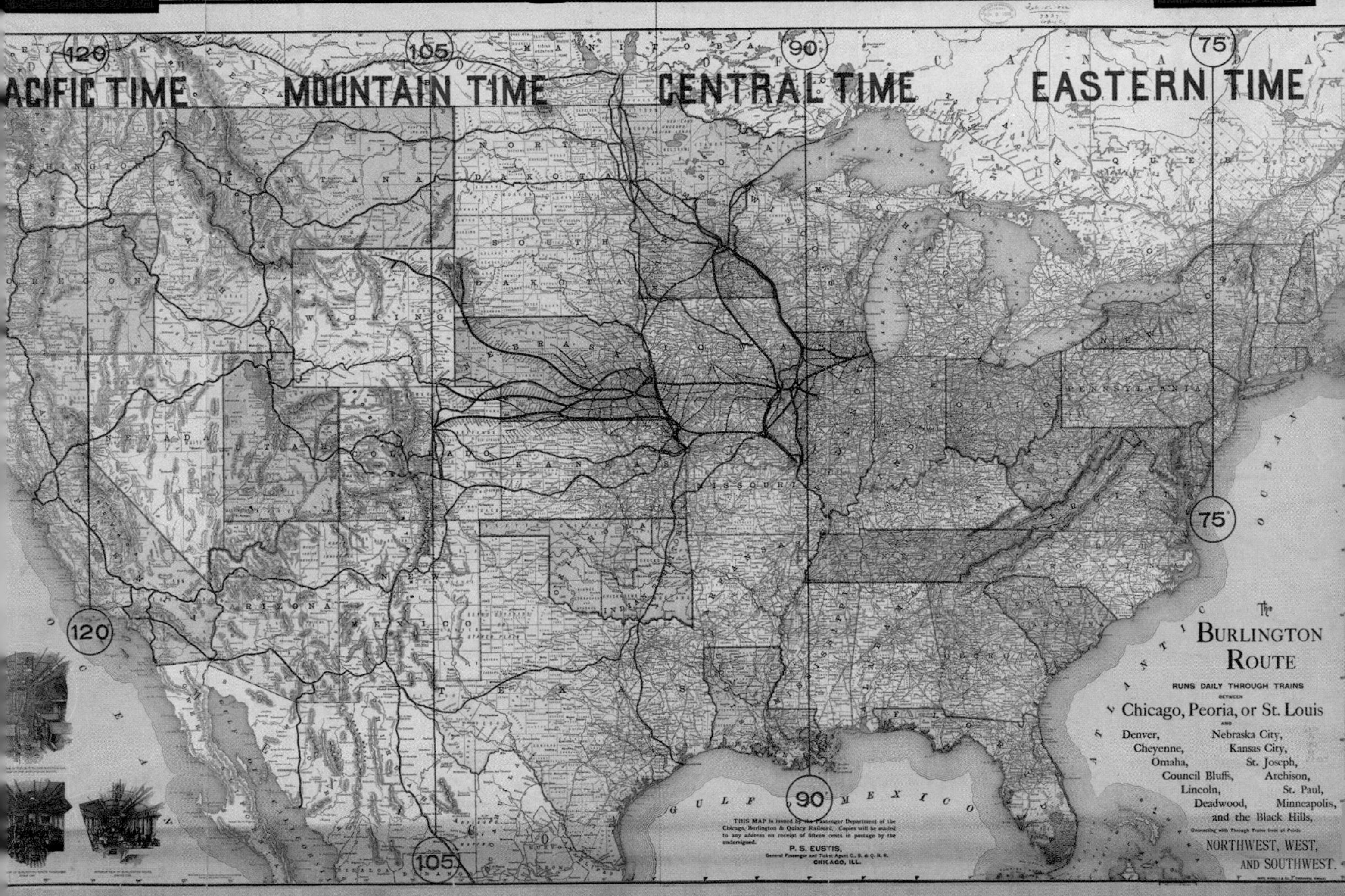

The US time zones shown here are from 1892. Today, the time zones divide up the country differently.

GMT AND UTC

The time zones are mostly based on **longitude**. In 1884, the longitude line passing through Greenwich, England, was established as the **Prime Meridian**. The time there—Greenwich Mean Time (GMT)—became the basis of the world's standard time. Today, the world's standard time is based on Coordinated Universal Time (UTC), which is the time zone Greenwich is in. **Atomic clocks** are used to keep the time exact.

There are 24 time zones on Earth. Time zones next to one another are commonly 1 hour apart.

JUST THE FACTS

*Lines of **latitude** and longitude are used on maps of Earth to help find places. They're measured in degrees. Each time zone is about 15 degrees of longitude, or 1/24 of Earth's total of 360 degrees.*

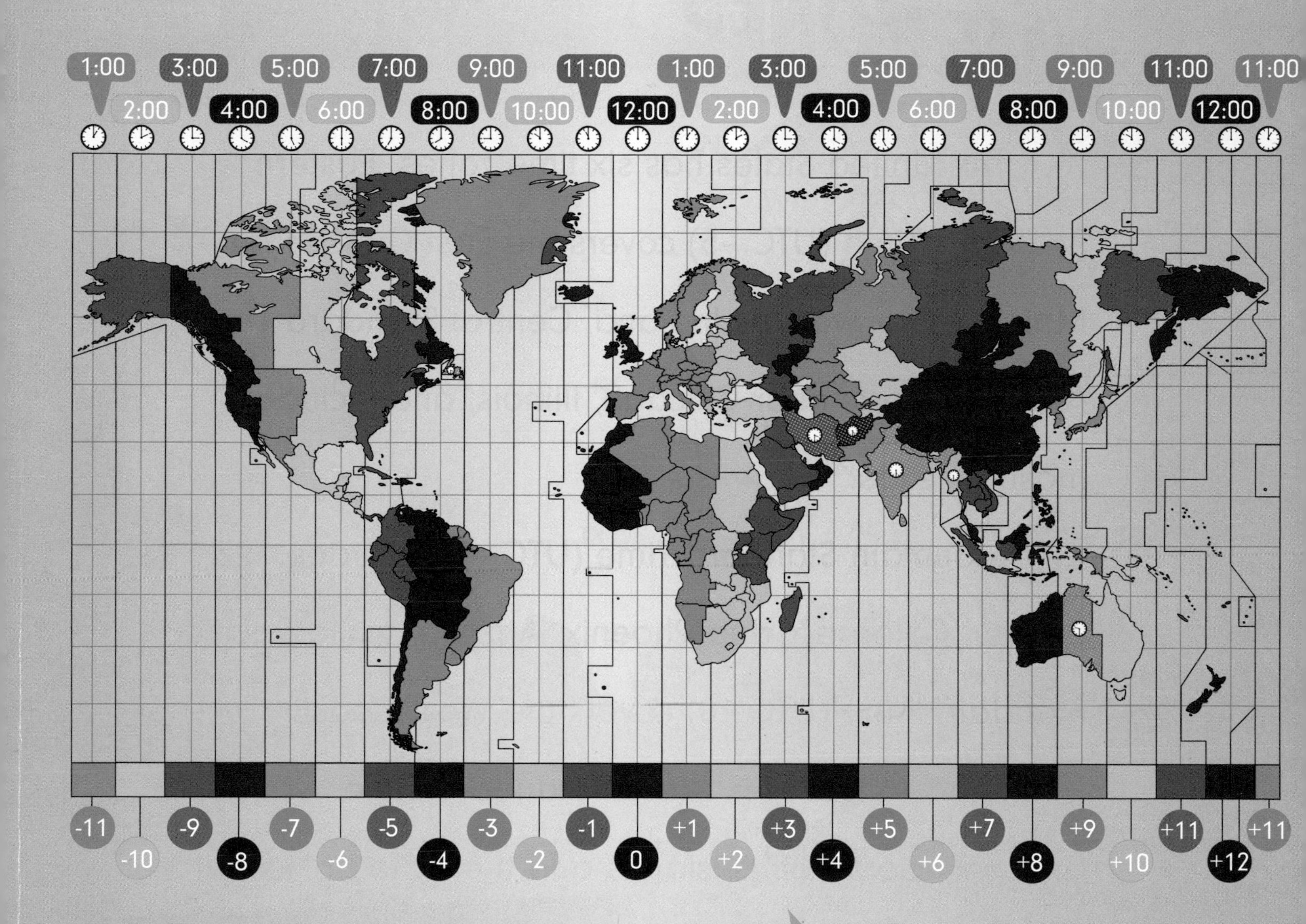

East of UTC, times zone are written with a + and a number to show how many hours ahead of UTC the time zone is. To the west, they're written with a – and a number to show how many hours behind UTC the time zone is. These are shown at the bottom of this map.

DAYLIGHT SAVING

Daylight Saving Time (DST) is a way to give people more waking daylight hours during the spring and summer. Most of the United States and European countries observe DST. Others, such as many countries in Africa and some in Asia, don't.

During DST, clocks are set forward 1 hour in the spring. Clocks then fall back to standard time in the fall. DST starts in March or April and ends between September and November in the Northern **Hemisphere**. It's the opposite in the Southern Hemisphere.

JUST THE FACTS

During DST, the time of a place will commonly be just 1 hour different from the standard time of that time zone. But since not every country observes DST, places in the same time zone will be on different times. This can cause problems!

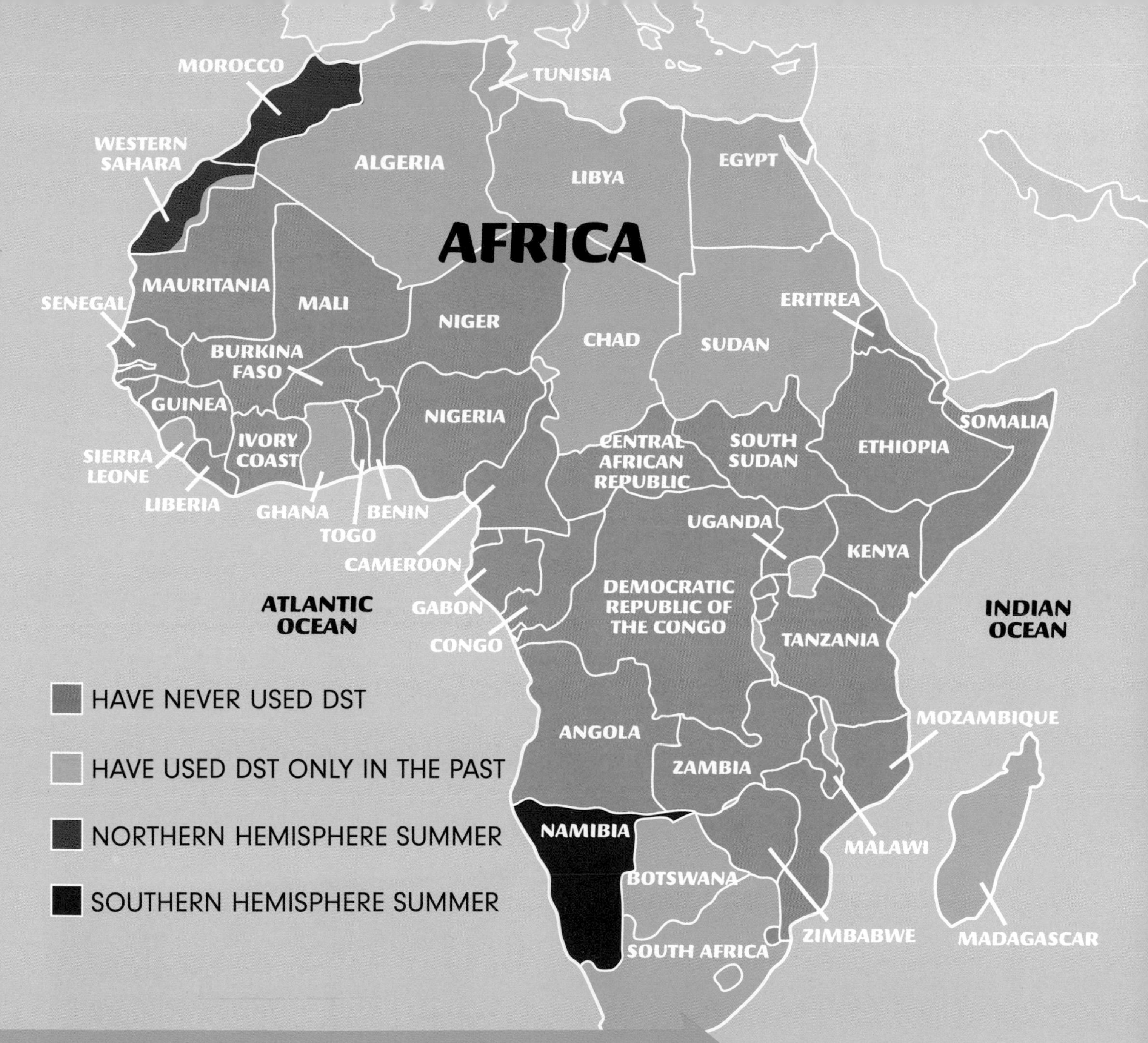

Most African countries don't use DST today. Morocco and Western Sahara are north of the equator and follow Northern Hemisphere DST. Namibia is south of the equator and follows Southern Hemisphere DST.

WACKY TIME ZONES

Time zones aren't always 15 degrees of longitude wide. They're changed to benefit major cities and fit countries' irregular shapes. Some countries even change their standard time by 15 or even 30 minutes from standard UTC. India is UTC +5:30!

Because of how the time zones were drawn, Kiribati, a country in the Pacific Ocean, was once divided by the **International Date Line**. One side was a day and 2 hours behind the other! In 1995, Kiribati changed to one time zone.

JUST THE FACTS

We even use the time zones in space! The International Space Station (ISS) is considered to be in Coordinated Universal Time.

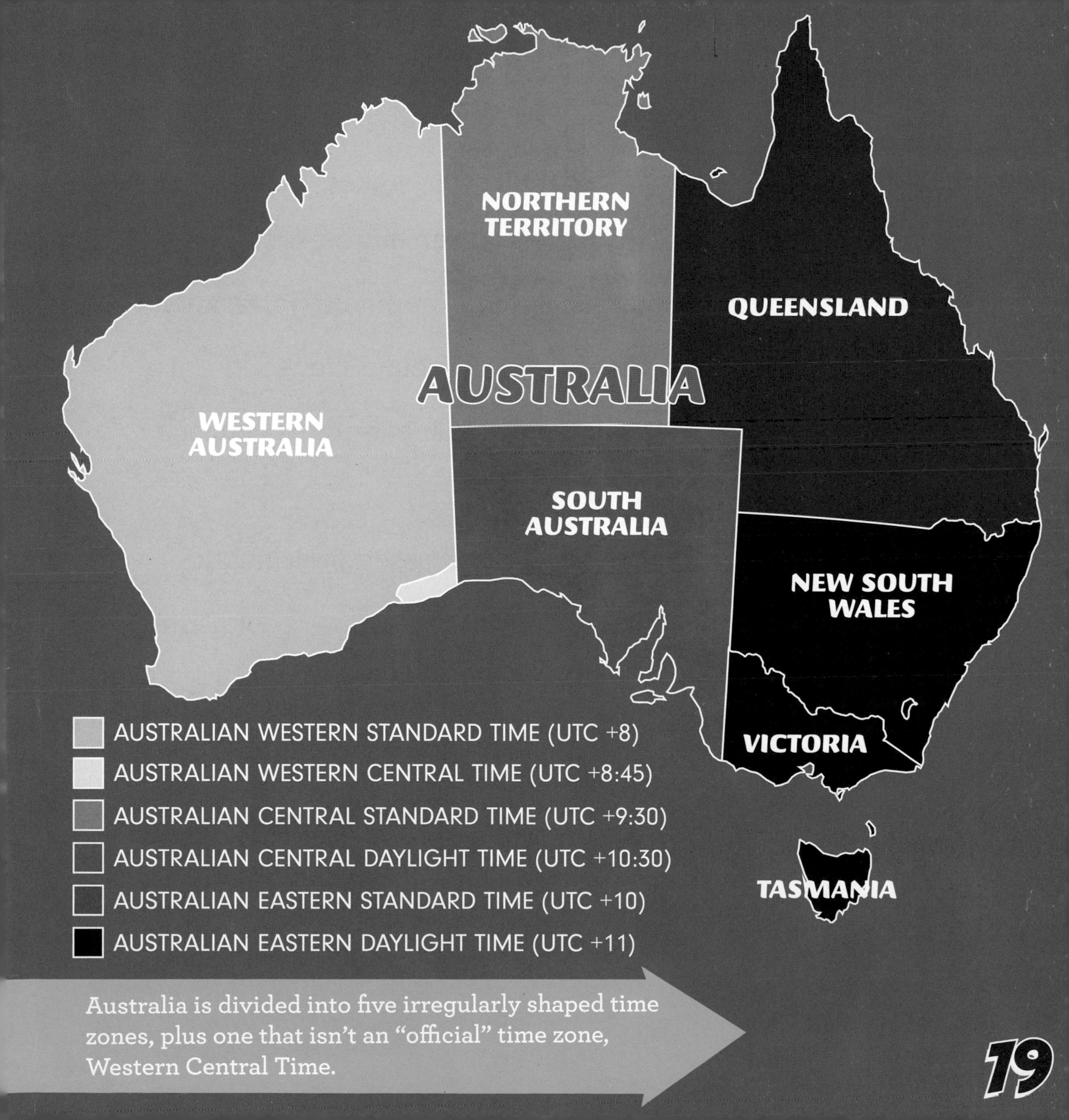

Australia is divided into five irregularly shaped time zones, plus one that isn't an "official" time zone, Western Central Time.

KEEPING TIME

Telling time has become even more exact in recent years. Atomic clocks can keep near-perfect time for millions of years! People all around the world base their clocks off the same time, but time zones continue to change to make life easier.

In 2014, people in India discussed switching to two different time zones. Scientists say they could save billions of units of electricity by changing the clocks just 30 minutes. How else will time zones change in years to come?

JUST THE FACTS

Midway Island, a US territory, and Anadyr, Russia, are 23 hours apart despite being on the same line of longitude!

GLOBAL TIME ZONES

WHEN IT'S NOON IN UTC, WHAT TIME IS IT ELSEWHERE?

PLACE	TIME
Los Angeles, California	4:00 a.m. (UTC -8)
New York City	7:00 a.m. (UTC -5)
Sao Paulo, Brazil	10:00 a.m. (UTC -2)
London, England	12:00 p.m. (UTC)
Paris, France	1:00 p.m. (UTC +1)
Cairo, Egypt	2:00 p.m. (UTC +2)
Moscow, Russia	4:00 p.m. (UTC +4)
Mumbai, India	5:30 p.m. (UTC +5:30)
Jakarta, Indonesia	7:00 p.m. (UTC +7)
Manila, Philippines	8:00 p.m. (UTC +8)
Shanghai, China	8:00 p.m. (UTC +8)
Tokyo, Japan	9:00 p.m. (UTC +9)

GLOSSARY

atomic clock: an extremely exact clock that uses the natural vibrations of atoms to measure time

global: having to do with the whole world

hemisphere: one half of Earth

International Date Line: the longitude line established as the start of the calendar day

latitude: the imaginary lines that run east and west above and below the equator

longitude: the imaginary lines that run north and south to the left and right of the Prime Meridian

pendulum: a weighted stick that swings back and forth at a regular rate

Prime Meridian: the line of longitude at 0 degrees from which other lines of longitude are measured

schedule: a list of times when trains, planes, or buses will leave

FOR MORE INFORMATION

BOOKS

Adler, David A. *Time Zones.* New York, NY: Holiday House, 2010.

Omololu, Cynthia Jaynes. *When It's Six O'Clock in San Francisco: A Trip Through Time Zones.* Boston, MA: Clarion Books, 2009.

WEBSITES

Time Zone Converter
timeanddate.com/worldclock/converter.html
Find out the time difference between cities around the world with this site.

Time Zones
wonderopolis.org/wonder/why-do-we-have-different-time-zones/
Read more about times zones on this website just for kids.

INDEX